A Note to Parent

Dorling Kindersley Readers is [ ] programme for children, designed in conjunction with leading literacy experts, including Cliff Moon M.Ed., Honorary Fellow of the University of Reading. Cliff Moon has spent many years as a teacher and teacher educator specializing in reading and has written more than 140 books for children and teachers. He reviews regularly for teachers' journals.

Beautiful illustrations and superb full-colour photographs combine with engaging, easy-to-read stories to offer a fresh approach to each subject in the series. Each *Dorling Kindersley Reader* is guaranteed to capture a child's interest while developing his or her reading skills, general knowledge, and love of reading.

The four levels of *Dorling Kindersley Readers* are aimed at different reading abilities, enabling you to choose the books that are exactly right for each child:

Level 1 – Beginning to read
Level 2 – Beginning to read alone
Level 3 – Reading alone
Level 4 – Proficient readers

The "normal" age at which a child begins to read can be anywhere from three to eight years old, so these levels are intended only as a general guideline.

No matter which level you select, you can be sure that you are helping children learn to read, then read to learn!

www.dk.com

Project Editor Penny Smith
Designer Michelle Baxter
Senior Editor Linda Esposito
Managing Art Editor Peter Bailey
Production Josie Alabaster
Picture Research Christine Rista
Natural History Consultant
Colin McCarthy

Reading Consultant
Cliff Moon M.Ed.

Published in Great Britain by
Dorling Kindersley Limited
9 Henrietta Street
London WC2E 8PS

2 4 6 8 10 9 7 5 3 1

A CIP catalogue record for this book is
available from the British Library.

ISBN 0-7513-5858-4

Colour reproduction by Colourscan, Singapore
Printed and bound in China by L Rex

The publisher would like to thank the following
for their kind permission to reproduce their photographs:
a=above; c=centre; b=below/bottom; l=left; r=right; t=top

Bruce Coleman Ltd: Gunter Ziesler 26–27;
John Cancalosi 28; John Visser 22, 23t; MPL Fogden 21cl;
Rod Williams 16–17; **N.H.P.A.:** Anthony Bannister 24b;
Daniel Heuclin 18, 29t; KH Switak 14;
Oxford Scientific Films: Alastair Shay 3, 20;
Planet Earth Pictures: Brian Kenney 12;
Warren Photographic: Jane Burton 9b

DORLING KINDERSLEY *READERS*

Slinky, Scaly Snakes!

Written by Jennifer Dussling

DK

London • New York • Sydney • Delhi • Paris • Munich • Johannesburg

Slinky, scaly snakes
slide along the ground.

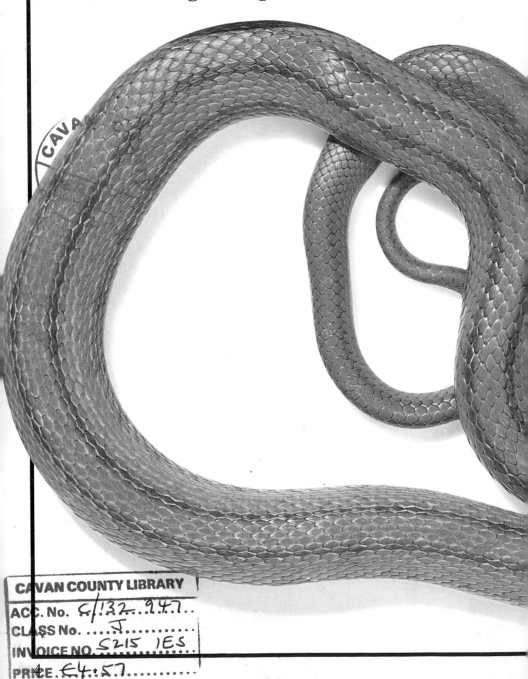

They have no legs and
they never blink their eyes.

Everglades rat snake

Snakes are shiny and
can look slimy.
But they are dry and
smooth to touch.

Rattlesnake

A snake's whole body
is covered in scales
that are hard and tough
like fingernails.

Snakes grow quickly but
their skin doesn't stretch.
When a snake's skin gets too tight,
the snake has to shed it.
This is called sloughing (sluff-ing).

Rock python

The snake rubs its head
on something rough like a log.
After a few minutes,
the skin begins to peel.

*The shed skin
of a snake*

The snake slides forward
right out of its skin!
Underneath is a new skin
which looks bright and shiny.
The snake keeps on growing.
Soon it will be time
to slough again.

Wait and see

When a snake is ready
to slough, its eyes turn
milky white. The snake
is almost blind for a week,
so it stays hidden.

Snakes move along the ground
in long, slinky curves.
The ground may look smooth but
it has little bumps everywhere.
A snake pushes off the bumps
to move itself forward.

The sidewinder snake
lives in the desert.
It throws itself forward
one part at a time.
It leaves behind
wavy-looking tracks.

Eyelash viper

Not all snakes live on the ground – some live in trees.

Snakes may not have legs,
but they can still climb.
The scales on a snake's belly
are larger than
the ones on its back.
These scales grip the tree.

The snake uses
its strong muscles
to pull itself up the tree.

Boa constrictor

13

How are snakes born?
Some give birth to live babies.
Other snakes lay eggs.

Florida kingsnake laying eggs

Soft shell

Snake eggs are not hard like chicken eggs.
The shells are soft – almost like leather.

A mother snake doesn't usually stay with her eggs.

She lays them in a soft, warm place, then she leaves them.

Soon a baby snake pokes its head out of the egg.

Then it slithers out of its shell.

Rat snake

Haitian (HAY-shun) boa

This snake is not moving.
Only its tongue flicks in and out.
It is checking for danger.

Most snakes can't see
or hear very well but
they have a strong sense of smell.
And they pick up these smells
with their tongues.

A fox meets a whipsnake

But what are snakes afraid of?
Hawks, raccoons and foxes
like to eat snakes.
Some snakes eat other snakes.
But many snakes have ways
to fool their enemies.

Some snakes blend in
with the area around them.
This vine snake looks like
a vine hanging from a tree.

These gaboon vipers
look like fallen leaves.

Other snakes try to trick
their enemies.

The parrot snake
opens its mouth very wide and
tries to look scary.

The milk snake is harmless.
But it looks like
the deadly coral snake,
so animals stay away.

Coral snake

Milk snake

The grass snake has a great trick.
When an enemy is near,
it plays dead!

All snakes are meat-eaters.
Small snakes eat small animals
like insects, lizards and worms.
Some snakes eat eggs.
This snake is swallowing a bird's egg.

Egg-eating snake

The egg makes a huge bulge
in the snake's body.

The egg breaks inside the snake.
Then the snake spits out the shell.

A rat makes a tasty meal
for a boa constrictor.

First the snake grabs the rat.
The snake holds on fast
with its strong jaws.

Tight squeeze
Snakes crush their prey but
they don't break bones.
They squeeze just enough
to make the animal
stop breathing.

It wraps its long body
round and round the rat.
Then the snake starts to squeeze
tight . . . tighter . . . tighter.
Soon the rat's heart stops.

The snake opens its mouth
very, very wide.
It gulps once or twice and
swallows the rat head first.

A rock python swallowing a Thomson's gazelle

Big snakes eat bigger animals.
Giant pythons and boas
can be as long as a school bus.
They eat pigs, goats and gazelles.

Big eaters

A meal can last
a long time.
Snakes like this python
have gone a whole year
without eating!

Mojave rattlesnake

Many snakes use poison
to kill their food.
The poison is stored in sacs
close to their long, sharp fangs.

The snake sticks its fangs
into the animal.

*Uracoan
rattlesnake*

The poison shoots through the
fangs and into the animal's body.
It does not take long
for the animal to die.
Then the snake swallows it whole.

Born to kill

A cobra can kill from
the minute it is born.
Just one tablespoon
of its dried poison
can kill 160,000 mice!

Can snakes hurt people?
Many can.
Here are some snakes
that can poison people.

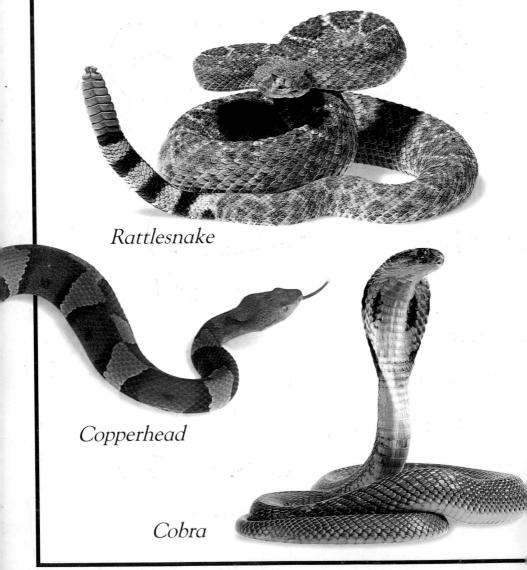

Rattlesnake

Copperhead

Cobra

But if people are bitten,
snakes can help!
Medicine is made from their poison
to treat snake bites.

Biting people better
A snake bites through the
thin covering
over a container.
Poison dripping from
its fangs is collected.

Snakes are useful in lots of ways.
They eat millions of mice and
other pests.
And they are eaten
by other hungry animals.
Our world would not be the same
without slinky, scaly snakes!

Snake Facts

Snakes are cold-blooded.
They lie in the sun to warm up
and move into the shade
to cool down.

Unlike people,
snakes never stop growing.

The world's heaviest snake
is the anaconda.
It can weigh as much
as three grown men.

The smallest snake
is the thread snake.
It is as skinny
as the lead in a pencil!

Baby snakes have a tooth
to help them break their eggs.
It falls off soon after they hatch.

It's not hard
to outrun a snake.
The fastest ones slither along
at the same speed as you walk.